MEGA TO. IPS:
DEALING WITH
CHALLENGING BEHAVIOUR

Sue Brown and Alice Langtree

Copyright © Scripture Union 2011
First published 2011
ISBN 978 1 84427 531 1

Scripture Union England and Wales
207–209 Queensway, Bletchley,
Milton Keynes, MK2 2EB, England
Email:info@scriptureunion.org.uk
Website: www.scriptureunion.org.uk

Scripture Union Australia
Locked Bag 2, Central Coast Business
Centre, NSW 2252
Website: www.scriptureunion.org.au

Scripture Union USA
PO Box 987, Valley Forge, PA 19482
Website: www.scriptureunion.org

Bible quotations have been taken
from the Contemporary English
Version © American Bible Society.
Anglicisations © British and Foreign
Bible Society 1996. Published by
HarperCollins Publishers and used
with permission.

The right of Sue Brown and Alice
Langtree to be identified as authors of
this work has been asserted by them
in accordance with the Copyright,
Designs and Patents Act 1988.

British Library Cataloguing-in-
Publication Data: a catalogue record
of this book is available from the
British Library.

Printed and bound by
Bell & Bain Ltd, Glasgow.

Logo, cover design, internal design:
www.splash-design.co.uk
Internal illustrations: Colin Smithson
Typesetting: Richard Jefferson, Author
and Publisher Services

❧ Scripture Union is an
international Christian charity working
with churches in more than 130
countries, providing resources to bring
the good news about Jesus Christ to
children, young people and families
and to encourage them to develop
spiritually through the Bible and
prayer.

As well as our network of volunteers,
staff and associates who run holidays,
church-based events and school
Christian groups, we produce a wide
range of publications and support
those who use our resources through
training programmes.

CONTENTS

INTRODUCTION

It's all about relationship. Some children have never learnt that an adult could love them unconditionally, help them change their troubled behaviour and go on loving them. To see something of this in an adult is the basis of knowing what a relationship with God could be like.

You've probably picked up this book because you have met with behaviour that worries you. Sometimes it's the child, at other times it's you! So, it's vital that each adult can manage their own 'challenging behaviour'. That means knowing yourself well enough to understand what might cause you to 'lose it' and consequently damage the relationship with the children you are with.

One key to staying calm – so that you can be firm, fair and flexible as you manage a child's behaviour – is understanding. All behaviour that seems difficult will have started by a conscious or unconscious threat in the child's mind. From 'naughtiness' in an able child, to self-harm or destructive behaviour in a vulnerable child, the root cause is a perceived threat. Lessening these threats by understanding how brains work and what our basic emotional needs are will mean that you can respond with confidence to each child.

A child who is confident in their relationship with you will learn to choose appropriate or good behaviours. This will hopefully result in praise and a further boost to self-esteem.

Pray for each child that has caused you to pick up a book like this... and then let's set to work together.

PART ONE – WHAT THE BIBLE SAYS

Before we get into the details of challenging behaviour, let's first take a look at what the Bible has to say on the subject. Thankfully, the Bible isn't an antiquated book that has nothing to do with our modern lives. Believe it or not, there are plenty of examples that are linked to challenging behaviour.

We are all capable of challenging behaviour

One of the most well-known verses that explains the human condition is found in Romans 3:23: 'All of us have sinned and fallen short of God's glory.' From the time of Adam and Eve onwards, every human being's behaviour has not been, and is not, up to God's standard. A well-known speaker was once heard to say that if you take all the sin out of the Bible, you would end up with a very thin book! The Bible is full of examples of behaviour (predominantly by adults) that is far from perfect:

- lashing out in anger or frustration (Moses, Numbers 20:10–12)
- lying about things (Abraham, Genesis 12:12–20)
- making too much noise (children at the Temple with Jesus, Matthew 21:15,16)
- fighting or arguing over who sits next to whom (the disciples, Matthew 20:20–24)
- willing to do anything to please others, even when you know it's wrong (Pontius Pilate, Mark 15:15)
- violence – and even murder (Moses, Exodus 2:12; David and Bathsheba's husband, 2 Samuel 11:14,15).

Think about...
Recall a time when, as a child, you behaved 'imperfectly'. What did you do? Why did you behave like that?

So, if the Bible is full of unhelpful behaviours, perhaps we shouldn't be surprised when, during our work, we too encounter actions that can be difficult to deal with.

Our world is damaged

At this point in our history we are stuck in the time that's described in Romans 8:22,23 like this: 'We know that all creation is still groaning and is in pain, like a woman about to give birth. The Spirit makes us sure about what we will be in the future. But now we groan silently, while we wait for God to show that we are his children.'

The world that we live in is sadly a long way from being perfect. It is full of imperfect people acting far from perfectly towards other imperfect people. This naturally affects the children and young people with whom we come into contact. It should come as no surprise to learn that young people who come from backgrounds of the greatest difficulty often have the greatest likelihood of suffering from a whole range of problems – including anti-social behaviour and mental health problems. It makes sense that if someone is struggling in one area of their life then their difficulties will 'leak' into another. So, for example, if a young person is being bullied at school they may find that the only time they can assert themselves (and possibly overly assert themselves) is during your midweek club.

As leaders, we also need to be aware of the effect the world is having on us and how it may impact on what we do. So if we are leading a trip out with our group, but we have had a

> **Think about...**
> How does what's happening in other areas of your life influence how you speak to the children, how organised you are and, of course, how enthusiastic you are?

essured week at work, we may find it more difficult to run that trip an if we had had a perfect week.

veryone is made in God's image

 spite of the above, we are all made in God's image. This may seem ovious but there can be times when, particularly if a child or young erson is being especially difficult, it could be easy to forget that this is ue. Although Genesis 1 and 2 make it clear that every person is made the image of God, it can sometimes feel that some children we meet ave had every bit of God squeezed out of them!

Ve always have a choice

ght from the start of creation, God gave people a choice: 'The oman answered, "God said we could eat fruit from any tree in the arden, except the one in the middle. He told us not to eat fruit from at tree or even to touch it. If we do, we will die."' (Genesis 3:2,3)

We and those we work with always have choices. In some cases, e's circumstances and pressures can make it very difficult to make the ght choice – but the option still remains.

The child who is acting up in your group in order to look good to eir friends can still make a choice to stop doing what they are doing. he young person who is withdrawn and upset can choose to take up e offer of a chat with someone who is working with them. A child n choose to engage in some of the 'win–win' strategies suggested ter in this book (page 38), or to reject them.

It's also worth remembering how God responds when people end making the wrong choices. He doesn't withdraw the option to oose, or his mercy and love. We, too, need to make sure that we

don't use our power as authority figures to remove free will from thos
we work with. Our times with young people should never be about
them being ordered to think, do and believe certain things. Free will
and choice should always be central.

Our responsibility as leaders

Of course, allowing children to have the freedom to choose doesn't
mean that it's OK to allow them to do whatever they want, whenever
they want. Imagine for a minute what the consequences of that migh
be!

Parents or the main carers of a child are the ones who are ultimate
responsible for their upbringing. However, for the times that children c
young people are attending something we are running, it is up to us t
take on a parental type of role and to treat them as God calls parents
to treat their children. The word for parent in the following verses also
means 'one in authority': 'Children must always obey their parents. Th
pleases the Lord. Parents, don't be hard on your children. If you are,
they might give up.' (Colossians 3:20,21)

These verses show a two-way respectful relationship. Children are
told to do what the person in authority says. However, those in
authority should work hard not to overdo the 'in authority' bit as this
could cause the young person to give up (literally, 'become spiritless').
So any authority used when working with children or young people
should not be the sort that kicks the life or spirit out of them.

Another part of the Bible that speaks about the way authority shoul
be worked out is Ephesians 6. The first three verses again tell children t
obey their parents – because then they will please God and lead a
happier life. Verse 4 says: 'Parents, don't be hard on your children. Rais
them properly. Teach them and instruct them about the Lord.'

The words 'teach and instruct' have the sense of 'cherish, train and nourish'. In the original language the verse had an implication of training, educating and disciplining.

So what can we, as leaders of young people, learn from what the Bible says to parents? First, it isn't wrong for us to expect young people to do what we ask. However, we are in a privileged position of being in a place of authority with children and we need to ensure that we do not misuse that authority in a way that crushes them or abuses their free will. Our role is to train, instruct, care for and nurture them. Yes, it's more than OK to set clear boundaries on what sorts of behaviour are or are not acceptable. Young people need these in order to achieve and be the best they can. However, in all we do, the bottom line is love and care for those we work with. Only in the context of mutual respect can things like boundaries and rules work.

The best example

If we are looking for an example on how to work best with challenging young people, we need look no further than Jesus' interactions with his disciples! Here we see a group of men from a wide range of backgrounds (which at times might have been like having two sets of opposing football supporters in the same room), eager to follow Jesus but not always getting things right.

He took them to one side and explained things

After telling the parable of the sower (Mark 4), Jesus took the disciples to one side and explained the meaning of the parable to them. Although Jesus seemed to take this approach quite often, it seems as if the disciples still didn't understand what he was telling them! Yet Jesus still kept on explaining what was happening and why (for example,

Mark 10:32–34) – knowing and trusting that one day God would help all the disciples to understand.

When we are working with children and young people, it's essential that we too explain why we are doing certain things or asking some things of them. There is no point excluding someone from your group if you don't take them to one side and calmly explain why. There isn't much point in having rules if you don't work through with the group why such rules should be there and the benefits of them. Just like the disciples, they may not 'get it' at first. Keep on explaining, no matter how many times it takes, and keep trusting God to make things clear at some point.

Jesus also spent time with his disciples away from the crowds and the 'work' of his ministry. If we want children and young people to engage with God then it's essential that we are willing to spend time with them that isn't purely focused on teaching them something. The most life-changing work is often that which is relationally based. This is why 'drop-in' or 'chill-out' groups can be so valuable. They provide a safe space where people can go and just be themselves and get to know you (and vice versa).

He was honest with them

Although a common portrayal of Jesus is of one who is meek and mild, blessing little children, he often told it straight to the disciples! This doesn't exactly sound like some children's workers' softly-softly approach to dealing with challenging behaviour! However, Jesus' straight talking needs to be seen in the wider context of his relationship with the disciples. This was so strong that he could at times just tell them they were downright wrong! This doesn't give us licence to shout at anyone whenever we feel like it, but it does give us scope to be honest and tell children if they are wrong – in the context of still accepting them and caring for them no matter what.

Into practice…

We've looked here at a few of the many things that the Bible teaches us about challenging behaviour. But what about in our day-to-day contact with children and young people? How can we relate what we know from the Bible to the more recent understandings and theory about why challenging behaviour can sometimes occur. That's what the next section is all about. Let's put the theory into practice…

Think about…
Think of a particular child who you find difficult:
- How do the Bible verses in this section help in thinking about how to deal with their challenging behaviour?
- What can you learn from the way in which Jesus dealt with people?

PART TWO – THEORY INTO PRACTICE

2

1 HOW OUR BRAINS WORK

The Bible tells us a lot about the human condition and principles for dealing with children. However, it's also helpful to think about what modern theory can tell us about the causes of some challenging behaviour. If we understand that, then we are far more likely to respond in a helpful way. We can also become more aware of our own responses when faced with difficult situations. So first, some information on how brains work!

Basic ideas

A human brain is like a series of computers operating together, each section working in a set order. The technical terms are:
- The *thalamus*. This is the 'lookout' bit of our brains which monitors incoming sensory information – sound, sight, taste, movement or smell.
- The *limbic* system. This identifies memories of previous similar situations.
- The *prefrontal cortex*. This processes information and thinks through our responses.

Responding to physical needs

The thalamus: a child is prompted initially by basic physical needs such as hunger, pain or cold. This need may not be consciously identified but may trigger disruptive behaviour.

In reality…

A children's club struggled constantly with bad behaviour from the children. The club was based in a community house in the middle of a very deprived council estate. Over time, the group leaders realised that many of the children had not had an evening meal before (and probably wouldn't get an evening meal after) the club. The leaders began to provide a basic cooked tea for the children. This also provided time and space to chat to the children, behaviour improved and attendance levels went up!

Think about…

What specific times can you think of when your group is grumpy and squabbles (for example, when everyone's hungry before lunch).

Responding to old memories

Information arrives from the thalamus to the limbic system. This is the part of the brain that regulates emotions, memory and movement. If the limbic system identifies a situation in the memory that is similar to the new one, and the previous one was threatening to the child, a 'fight or flight' reaction may be triggered. The child may become challenging, stop joining in or run off.

Using our brains to think it through

The prefrontal cortex is the 'thinking' part of the brain, which starts to process what is happening. It makes decisions to limit 'fighting' behaviour or the impulse to run away. Children using this bit of their brains can differentiate between conflicting thoughts and choose good actions. They can engage with Bible stories and understand more of how much God loves them.

In reality...

The children came together for a Bible story, but Ryan ran off and hid under a table. As he was safe and not distracting anyone, the leader left him but kept an eye on him. At the end she praised everyone including Ryan: 'I was pleased that Ryan listened to the story.'

A child might feel threatened by being in a large group, not understanding an instruction, not wanting to stop a previous activity or not feeling valued. The following session she showed Ryan a circle of carpet and said, 'This is your safe place for storytime.' She gave a two-minute warning before the storytime and the change of activity. As she called Ryan to sit on his piece of carpet, she signed the words 'come' and 'sit' with her hands to help his understanding. Ryan is now very attached to his 'safe' carpet.

Consistent, caring relationships with committed volunteers leave good memories and enable a child to learn to control 'fight or flight' urges and decide on better behaviours.

When it doesn't quite work

Some children with disabilities will have impairment in these parts of the brain. For example, children on the autistic spectrum will have high levels of anxiety and may suffer from hypersensitivity. It is important to have clear structures and ways of enabling these children to feel safe and not threatened. Children with an attention deficit disorder may have damage to this part of the brain and need help to learn to manage and lessen their impulsive behaviours. (More information on children with additional needs can be found in Chapter 6.)

Identifying our reponses

If, as leaders, we feel threatened we may become disheartened and want to give up, or we may become angry at the child's behaviour. Sometimes it can be appropriate to pretend to be angry in dealing with a young person's behaviour but if we are *really* angry we may not be using our 'thinking' brain. The young person will sense our genuine anger as a threat and this may escalate the situation ('fight'). Alternatively, they may behave through fear ('flight') which may spoil relationships.

Understanding what triggers a child's behaviour and learning strategies for dealing with it builds a leader's confidence. Of course,

In reality...

On a residential holiday, Amy had opted out and was lying on her bed. A visitor had specifically come to run an activity, so the leader felt embarrassed that Amy refused to join in. The leader tried to talk with Amy but felt a failure as a leader. She resorted to telling Amy off sharply and their relationship disintegrated dramatically.

At the next meal, Amy looked fearfully at the leader. But the leader went across to her and asked Amy to forgive her. Amy was amazed at this. She had had so little experience of seeing relationships repaired. For the rest of the holiday, Amy and the leader worked well together and often joked about whether or not they were going to have another big row!

there will be times when we get it wrong. This presents an opportunity to model forgiveness and repair relationships, as both adult and child learn from one another.

Think about...
What are the situations that trigger your own 'fight or flight' reactions? How would you feel if a child swore at you or if a worksheet that had taken a lot of preparation was spoilt?

2 WHAT HUMAN BEINGS NEED

All human beings have complex needs. The theories about this can help us understand the young people we're working with and equip us to think about our responses to challenging behaviour.

What do we need?

We are born with a set of basic needs that need to be met in some way or other if we are to cope with the things that life invariably throws at us. Back in 1943 a man by the name of Abraham Maslow came up with a theory that many psychologists consider to be essential. Maslow's pyramid of human needs showed the order of needs that he believed people needed to have met. He thought that if a lower level was not being met then the higher up ones would only have, at best, a temporary usefulness. We've already hinted in Chapter 1 about some of the lower level needs that may bring about challenging behaviour, so let's look at them in a bit more depth here.

Think about...

As you read about each area of the pyramid, try to relate it to the group(s) you work with. Are these needs being met, and if so how? If they're not being met, what can you do to start this process rolling?

Maslow's pyramid of human needs

Here's a quick guide to what each level is about:

Staying alive and keeping safe

The bottom level on the pyramid means that the children you work with are clothed, well fed, are given medical attention when they need t etc. (For an example of how this could affect what you do, look at ɔage 14 in Chapter 1.)

The needs of the bottom two levels are pretty hard to separate. If ʋve want to reduce the chances of challenging behaviour then it's our ɔob to make sure that those who attend our activities feel safe there. ʲo, for example, if children or young people who come along to your ɡroup for the first time are expected to tell others personal information ɑbout themselves or do something like pray out loud then the environment can feel far from safe. Another way our clubs, Sunday or other activities can feel unsafe is to allow cliques to become dominant. Things like cliques can be reduced by mixing up members in activities and doing things together as a group.

One final, but essential, aspect of the bottom two levels is to ensure that what we do is physically safe. This means we need to ensure that leaders have had the appropriate police checks (so they can work with children), that we have clear boundaries for behaviour (see Chapter 5) and that we carry out risk assessments for all that we do.

> **Think about…**
> Is there any chance that someone who is disruptive in your group does so because they feel on the edge of things or threatened by what they are being asked to do?

Belonging and being loved

As Christians often say, each person is made with a God-shaped hole in them. Every human being, whether or not they know it, longs to be filled with God's love. God made people to be in relationships with

each other, to feel loved, cared for and have a place to belong. If all we do in our clubs is communicate God's love and acceptance of a child or young person, then we have done a good job.

Think about...
How does your club, activity or group communicate God's love? How successful are you? How could you improve?

In reality...
A Christian schools worker often found that he had to tell people to listen or ask them to stop doing something during a lesson. He learnt that a good approach was to walk over to the pupil and, with eye contact and in a quiet tone of voice, tell them to stop doing whatever it was they were doing. He would keep the eye contact for a second or two, then walk away and continue with the lesson. About a minute after this he would make a point of smiling at the whole class and then, making direct eye contact, smile at the pupil he'd spoken to. He hoped to communicate that although their behaviour was not acceptable he still liked that pupil as much as the rest of the class.

Feeling valued

Feeling valued is about taking every opportunity to build people up. It's about taking every chance we have to praise children and to tell them something positive about themselves. As Christians we have the great job of telling people, not what's wrong with them, but what is right about them.

There is also a need for many older children to feel they have a role in a group. If this is the case, then why not delegate out some of the jobs in your group? Most children will rise to this challenge and feel valued at the same time.

Reaching your full potential

The final level is about being secure and sure of who you are and what you believe. Having autonomy and control is about becoming whole as a person, being confident in making your own decisions, learning new knowledge and stepping out into the world as an independent person. Sadly, with unresolved issues, even many adults don't reach this stage in life.

What if these needs aren't met?

Children's early experiences with their main carer are possibly one of the greatest influences on their behaviour. Experts agree that the patterns of how people will behave and think throughout their life is in place by just two years of age. Now that's scary!

One of the people who have studied this idea is John Bowlby. He looked at the impact that the relationship between baby and main carer in the first two years of a child's life had on the child's behaviour later on.

His main idea was that, for a child to grow and develop in a way that enables them to cope with relationships and life's circumstances, they needed to have experienced (from birth onwards) a primary carer who has shown them consistent love.

Infants and young children learn quickly what they need to do to survive without this basic need of consistent love and attention being met. Challenging behaviour can arise because children and young people continue to use their early coping strategies beyond infancy. Here are three main types of behaviour that might result.

Those who don't like you

Infants who have not experienced a loving primary carer can develop into group members who don't seem to bond with you. Children or young people like this have learnt to survive by keeping people at a distance. Relationships are just downright dangerous to them. This could be marked by obvious hostility and challenges directly

aimed at you. They probably also won't have many, if any, close friendships. They have learnt to live life in a bubble where they don't need anyone else's help. It's easy to feel very rejected by these sorts of children and young people.

Think about...
How do you cope with someone in your group who doesn't seem to like you?

In reality...

One boy at the after-school club seemed very aggressive. When Clare went up to speak to him he reacted, stamping his feet and shouting that she was stupid. He lashed out and spilled paint all over the floor. During the craft time, Clare noticed that he had drawn a car. Clare handed him some extra pencils and he didn't react. Over the following weeks the boy was often very disruptive and Clare seriously considered whether to let him attend. However, she noticed that if she helped him with his craft, or gave him a job to do, he seemed a lot calmer. As the weeks and months went on, the boy seemed to settle down and even began to talk to Clare about the crafts he was doing.

Trying to build a relationship with them directly probably won't work. This is too threatening. You need to find an indirect way of doing this. One thing that isn't threatening is the task you are doing with them. During activities you can attempt to get alongside them by doing this with them. The thing you are doing becomes almost like a buffer between you and the child. By keeping the focus on the task, the child or young person will probably become less hostile to you and find the environment a more and more secure place.

Those who seem superglued to you!

At the opposite end of the spectrum, there are the children who think you are fantastic. It seems that wherever you go… there they are. They want your attention and won't be considerate of other group members in getting it. So, while trying to talk to someone else, they might well interrupt with a question for you. No matter how simple the task, they constantly want support from you. Children and young people like this

In reality…

John realised Kevin needed some extra support and so began to greet him at the door each week and got him to make drinks with him for everyone. Soon, Kevin seemed inseparable from John. He always sat next to him, wanted to know every detail of John's week and got angry when the other young people seemed to get more of John's attention. John got two other leaders to help him out. They began to draw some of the attention from John, taking turns to make the drinks with Kevin and chatting with him. Kevin didn't like this at first but after a while got used to it. John still had time for Kevin but he now had relationships with the wider team too.

can be quite draining. You may feel that others are getting neglected and that the whole group revolves round this person.

Once again, children and young people who display this kind of behaviour may not have experienced a loving primary carer in their infancy. In particular, a parent or main carer may not have been around for the time that the child needed. Children try to fill this gap by becoming 'clingy' towards adult figures who show an interest in them.

How to best work with a child or young person like this? To expect someone with this mindset to suddenly be able to be independent is not possible. However, the aim is to help them become less reliant on you. This can only be done in small steps. So, if you are doing a craft activity, you may want to explain the whole craft to the group then take the child to one side and explain the first section. Encourage them to come back to you for the next instruction when they have completed the first (and not before). Over time, increase the size of the instructions so that they become less reliant on you for every step.

Think about...
Is there a child in your group who constantly demands your attention? What strategies have you tried? How could other members of the team help?

Those who seem out of control

Thankfully, a very small percentage of the population seem out of control and many will have additional needs (see Chapter 6). These are the children and young people who are very unpredictable. One minute they may seem fine, the next they could be smashing things up, running in and out of the room, making no sense or even attacking others.

This group tend to come from the most difficult backgrounds. They are often the victims of abuse, excluded from school, refugees or asylum seekers (having witnessed traumatic events) or are in the care system (now known as 'looked-after children').

Most of their behaviour comes from fear – which is acted out as aggression. They are very sensitive to feeling they may be humiliated, and certain activities or actions can trigger their anti-social responses. Young people like this need:

- a safe space – somewhere they can go when they start to feel not so good;
- as much routine as possible;
- activities that don't make them feel exposed – games where they may lose, or doing something that you then have to show others could be unhelpful;
- the chance to opt out.

If a child or young person 'explodes', the first thing to do is not to react back. Take a step back (making the space around them feel more safe), keep speaking in the same tone, softer if possible, until they feel they can go to their safe space for as long as they need.

How can we meet the needs in our group?

Some ideas to try:
- give attention to good behaviour
- praise, praise, praise
- explain boundaries
- explain what's happening
- be creative (remember VAK: visual, audio, kinaesthetic)
- give jobs, responsibilities
- give choices.

Creativity and stimulation

Children and young people – especially those who are troubled – don't necessarily have the ability or even the desire to sit down and pour out their hearts to us. But something that most will want to do in some way is to express themselves. Use creativity and stimulation to help the young people in your group to do this.

Play can have a very important role. This isn't necessarily the sort of play where we prescribe a certain game, but the sort of play where they choose what to do and have the opportunity to be creative. This could be pouring paint onto paper and sloshing it all around (very therapeutic, in case you've never tried it!) or it could be acting out a scene with play figures where they can make the world into whatever they want it to be. By allowing this sort of creative play, children have the opportunity to get out of their systems the issues that may be troubling them.

Try some of these with children in your group:
- Invite children to choose a colour that expresses how they feel for different emotions (this can be as simple or complex as you want).

- Each week, in your group, give the opportunity to put out whatever colour card they are feeling that day onto the table. Let the children expand on it – or not.
- *Incentive Plus* (see Resources, page 79) provides excellent resources to open up discussions about emotions (try *The Big Book of Blob Feelings*).
- A pack of 'blob cards' (people shapes in different poses, such as one hiding behind a tree, looking excited, falling down a hole etc) can be used as both an introduction to how they feel or as a prompt for prayer.

3 Children who are Hurting

The young people we work with live in a far from perfect world. Sadly, research shows that many young people today face immense difficulties that can potentially have a huge effect on them and their behaviour.

For example, in 2004 the Joseph Rowntree Foundation carried out a survey that found that 1 in 4 young people aged under 16 had experienced divorce or separation in their families.

Banardos compiled a survey in 2008 ('Don't give up on us') amongst young people, just over half of whom had been in trouble with the police or made the subject of anti-social behaviour orders (ASBOs). Most of those interviewed cited difficulties (such as family problems, being bullied, feeling lonely or scared) as major reasons for young people getting into trouble. Sixty-six per cent said they thought that more intervention when they were younger to keep them away from troublesome behaviour would help stop young people getting into trouble.

Many other pieces of research have shown that massive numbers of young people do face real difficulties in their lives:

- One million 5–16 year olds have a diagnosable mental health disorder (The Children's Society, *The Good Childhood Inquiry*, 2006–2008).
- One in four children who have a faith are bullied because of it (Beatbullying, *Interfaith Report*, 2008).
- Children and young people who don't wear right brands mark are classed as 'geeks' and are the subject of bullying (Association of Teachers and Lecturers, quoted in the *Daily Mail* and the *Daily Telegraph*, 2008).

- 69 per cent of children are bullied at school, one quarter of young people are bullied via text or internet, 42 per cent of young people who truant at school are also bullied.

There can be no doubt that a very large number of young people are hurting and are damaged. This can then be expressed by challenging behaviour.

Loss

Loss is something that every child and young person faces in some way or other and the impact of this can show itself in the form of challenging behaviour.

Divorce or family separation

The whole area of divorce and family separation can bring up many reactions that may or may not be seen at home, but may be seen in the work you do with children and young people. Most of those identified in the Joseph Rowntree Foundation study were unhappy during and

after the separation. Many suffered from low self-esteem and struggled to cope. They also said that they 'acted out' their unhappiness through bad behaviour. However, the same study showed that if a child or young person encountered, through this process, a parent, carer or other responsible adult (such as their youth group leader) who would give them time to talk about and express their feelings, then most suffered no long-term damage.

However, for those who did not have an adult to help them through, many began to encounter problems relating to people generally and struggled to form positive relationships in adulthood. The message to us here is very clear – by just being there for those we know whose family structures are changing, we can change the course of the child or young person's life for the better.

Think about...
What major difficulties are individual young people in your group experiencing? How is that affecting their behaviour? Think about strategies for working with them helpfully and lovingly.

There are other dimensions to the break-up of families. In many ways, divorce and separation are almost like a bereavement and, because of their own pain, many parents struggle to support their children as much as they might want. Some families may be truly at war with each other, with the sons and daughters used as ammunition. And then, of course, there is the possible introduction of a new family, with stepbrothers and stepsisters. What was once stable and known to a child or young person suddenly becomes very different. The dynamics change and they can be left struggling with a range of emotions.

Bereavement

Experts have found that a child's response to grief can vary according to age. Although the responses may be different, it is important that we get alongside that person at whichever stage they may be. The main thing with grief is to not hurry it along, wanting a quick solution and relief for those involved. It may take years for someone to reveal their underlying feelings about their loss. It can also be very natural for someone who has lost someone to become angry at God or disillusioned with Christianity. Several months after a bereavement, a

In reality...

When he was 5 years old, Steven lost his dad in a car crash. His Sunday School leaders did all they could to help him, showing him lots of extra attention, but he continued to be withdrawn. About a year later, the Sunday School group were playing a game and Steven's side lost. One of the boys blamed Steven and Steven punched him then ran out of the room crying. One of the leaders ran after him. She asked him what was wrong and Steven blurted out that everything was his fault – including his dad's death. Steven had stored up this guilt for a year. The love and care shown to him by the leaders made it safe for him to share, when he could cope with it, his deepest guilt.

hild may start to become very disruptive in your group – attempting to undermine everything you do. It would be very natural in this situation especially if they hadn't immediately started to behave badly after the death) to deal with and focus primarily on the behaviour. However, in these instances it's important to respond, not react. We need to look beyond the behaviour to any underlying causes. What appears to be just a naughty and rude child may be a child shaking their fist at what they believe is a God who has taken away someone close.

Transition

The move from home to school and primary to secondary school are major points of loss and change for children. Both involve a movement away from what they have learnt to be a safe environment into a totally new and alien one. As children prepare to move to secondary or middle school, many are excited but many feel real sadness as they realise that they won't be around their old teachers and friends any more. Nor will they be the oldest in the school. They will be the youngest and therefore potentially the most vulnerable. Rumours of what happens at secondary school (most of which not very nice) are rife. All this provides a perfect recipe for some very insecure children and, therefore, potentially, some acting out of these things via challenging behaviour.

As in other areas, the best thing a group leader can do in this situation is to talk about the 'elephant in the room'. Scripture Union provides an excellent resource called *It's Your Move*, which can be used to help children work through what it means to move up to secondary school. There is also a fantastic pack called *Ready, Steady, Go!* for children moving to school for the first time. This pack is aimed at parents and children (both of whom will experience a sense of loss).

So, what can help?

Being there

The most important thing we could ever do to help any child or young person who has challenging behaviour is simply to be there. Children and young people are used to be branded and rejected when they behave in a less than perfect way. As Christians, we can show that there is a different way. This way doesn't mean that we accept their behaviour but it does mean that we look at whether there are underlying issues that may be causing it. Regardless of what our ideas are on this, we need to follow the example of Jesus himself who came to save sinners – less than perfect people. This means that we never ever give up on someone – no matter how challenging this may be!

A place for healing

Challenging behaviour can often be the tip of an iceberg. Underneath can be a vast number of reasons why someone is behaving as they are. A psychologist by the name of Carl Rogers did a lot of work with people who were struggling in one way or another. Thankfully, he did find a way to help people and it is one that doesn't require a training course to put into practice! Carl found that if you created the right environment for a child, young person (or adult) then many underlying difficulties, and the resulting challenging behaviours, improved. This 'right environment' includes:

Caring for the child or young person and valuing them – no matter what they do. Another way to put this would be to have unconditional love – just as God has for us.

Trying to see life through the eyes of the person you are working with – just as Jesus did when he walked on the earth.

Being real with the child or young person – not putting on an act or pretending to be something you're not.

Having the courage to look at why you react as you do to their behaviour.

This approach requires a long-term commitment. It means sticking with a young person even when their behaviour is unhelpful either to you or others. It can be an incredible challenge but it can also lead to amazing breakthroughs.

4 CONFLICT

Every one of us is different, and so there is bound to be conflict when we get together. Children will have experienced conflict between their parents, at school with other children or with teachers, and some may have learned that 'win–lose' is what happens when they show disagreement.

In Galatians 5 Paul points out that telling someone to behave and adding more and more rules is not an effective way to stop bad behaviour. Self-confidence comes from a feeling of being loved and results in a child choosing to behave well and act thoughtfully to others by looking for ways to find 'win–win' solutions. As William Glasser, the American psychiatrist, says (in *The Quality School*, Harper & Roe, 1990), 'The only person's behaviour we can control is our own.' Our challenge is to help the child to control their own behaviour.

Relationship is key to this, overcoming a child's underlying fear and showing that the adult next to them can be trusted. Research into this has shown that:

- 40 per cent of impetus for positive change is from the child themselves;
- 30 per cent of change is achieved through the relationship with the listener.

Dealing with conflict

If potential conflict is seen as a threat, a child can be triggered into a 'fight or flight' reaction, provoking fearful or angry behaviour. This is learned behaviour that is used because experience has shown that it works.

If a child's behaviour is dangerous to their own safety or that of others then it needs to be managed immediately. Stay calm, repeat your request firmly, clearly and simply, for example 'stop now' or 'put that down', remove other children, keep your distance and call for another adult. Only use physical restraint if you have been trained to do so.

These strategies are only a short-term response. A child may need to be shown how to understand and manage their reactions. If adults in the child's life are modelling angry behaviour, they, too, will feel better as they think about what 'winds them up' and use strategies and prayer to increase self-control, one of the fruits of the Holy Spirit.

Good anger diffusers are:

- distraction
- change of place
- change of activity
- humour
- active listening
- active ignoring.

Some confrontations are provoked by an adult picking up on a muttered rude comment rather than choosing to actively ignore a smaller issue in order to focus on a child joining in the main activity.

A child who is troubled and often gets angry can be taught some self-calming techniques, but not while they are still agitated. A child can learn to spot what is a 'wind-up' and then take positive calming action, such as:

- breathing in through their nose and out through their mouth
- self-talk – 'I can stay cool'
- counting to ten
- rubbing thumbs against the inside of fingers
- walking away to sit in a designated place, perhaps a beanbag just for them.

Think about...

Read Gemma's story on the opposite page. How would you deal with a situation like this? What are the key points in how the leaders went about resolving this situation?

In reality...

Gemma ran out of the meeting screaming at everyone in the room, 'I hate this holiday, I wish I'd never come, I don't want to be here.' There was a stunned silence and then she was followed by one of the holiday leaders. When Gemma stopped running a loud altercation developed about ringing home to get her fetched. Another leader who had not dealt with the child's previous outbursts and so was not in a state of 'high alert' was able to swap with the leader and stay calm. After a time of just sitting next to her in silence, the leader acknowledged Gemma's feelings and said, 'I'm sorry you are feeling upset.'

She began to distract Gemma by commenting, 'Tell me about yesterday, I understand you went on a trip out of camp.' She then gave Gemma some control as she asked, 'Where shall we go to talk about this?' Gemma did not speak but led the adult to sit outside the prayer room. The leader was then able to suggest a positive ending to Gemma's outburst: 'When you feel better, you can decide what to do next.'

Gemma spent half an hour writing sentences alternately with the leader about their homes, hobbies etc. During this time it emerged how upset she felt over the death of a relative the previous year. She was able to write down strategies for when she felt 'her tummy going all tight' and ended by writing a prayer: 'Jesus, please help me to get through this and have a nice time at this holiday.'

Gemma was able to go back to the main group and the leaders caught her eye at regular intervals during the rest of the day with a smile and a 'thumbs up'. She stood up at a talent show in the evening and read a poem out, then grinned from ear to ear as children and adults all applauded her loudly.

Mediation

One approach to resolving conflicts between children is mediation. This will not work if a child is still angry – time out is needed before children can respect each other, begin to understand how others are feeling and get everyone's needs met without hurting other people.

When everyone involved is ready to talk, the following type of structure could be followed:

1   Bring the group together in a circle and explain the ground rules:
    - each person will be allowed to talk without interruption
    - we expect to find a solution
    - each child will agree to follow what is decided.

2   Give each child a chance to explain:
    - what has happened
    - who has been affected
    - different ways of doing things.

3   As the mediator:
    - teach manners by modelling them (manners are 'respect in action' Michael Grose, www.parentingideas.co.uk)
    - use each child's name
    - say 'please' and 'thank you'
    - let each child speak
    - be a good listener
    - feed back to each child, speaking to show that you have heard and clarify that you have understood
    - don't take sides
    - choose a way that everyone can live with
    - look for ways to avoid similar conflict in future
    - praise each child in the group for achieving a way forward.

Behaviour plans

If a child shows persistent difficult behaviour then it may be appropriate to think about setting up a behaviour plan to help them make progress in building positive relationships.

To make a behaviour plan you will need first to watch the child at different times. Make notes not only on what is unacceptable behaviour but also on what happened before the poor behaviour and what follows on afterwards. You may spot something that regularly triggers the difficult behaviour, or else you may realise that the behaviour is being inadvertently rewarded by, say, individual attention.

Once you have figured out the behaviour that you want to get rid of then think of a positive behaviour that you will aim to teach instead. The behaviour you want should be 'SMART', ie:

Specific

Measureable

Achievable

Realistic, and achievable within a certain

Time.

If you are to be successful with the behaviour plan, it is important to involve the child by chatting one-to-one regularly and negotiating not only the desired behaviour but also what rewards and sanctions could be part of this.

Sticker charts often make good rewards or else building up points for a whole group treat, which might be a DVD or something edible.

All adults need to agree to be consistent alongside you in this plan and, if possible, the other children will be effective if they agree to help the child remember and carry out the good behaviour.

Circle of friends

If the children in your group are willing to support one another, the 'circle of friends' technique can be used to promote good relationships.

Invite everyone to sit in a circle and establish that the children agree to participate. Choose a child and then invite each person in the circle to make a positive comment about that child.

This approach can change whole group dynamics and introduce a 'glass half full' attitude to difficulties. A practical example of its use can be seen in the story on page 43.

Think about...

Read Gary and Mike's story on the opposite page. How would you have dealt with people like Gary and Mike if they were part of a group you were leading?

In reality...

Gary and Mike came along to the holiday club together but they continually squabbled, spoiled each other's things and seemed unable to listen to instructions or a story. Because the other children were willing to help, the leader sat the children in a circle and used the 'circle of friends' technique. The leader started by talking positively about Gary and Mike, but addressed his words to the adult helper and the other children. 'I'm pleased that we have Gary and Mike in the group because they have good ideas about different games we might play. Gary is kind to David. Mike is helpful in putting the chairs away when we finish. Sometimes Gary and Mike need our help not to feel sad, so I'd like us each to say something to help.'

This attracted the boys' attention and they were able to sit separately, one next to each of the leaders. The other children showed wonderful kindness and insight as they showed themselves willing to change their thoughts about the boys. Individual children in the group made comments, talking about cool trainers and how it must feel when your mum starts to live with someone else's dad and you have to share your bedroom with a stepbrother you are not sure about.

Over time, as the boys felt cared about they began to find ways to compromise and build friendship with each other. The other children were used by God to help but also some were able to explore their own fears that one day their parents might argue and break up.

The leader's flexibility in putting relationships before programme content at that time was based on good knowledge of each child in the group, being confident that Gary and Mike would enjoy positive attention from the whole group and that the group were mature enough to achieve this.

Avoiding conflict

There are ways to be prepared so that conflict is less likely to be generated:

- Meet and greet children individually so that you can affirm them and become aware of any that are upset or restless. Some will bring emotional baggage from home; some will have had arguments with another child earlier or at school. Use helpers to give a distressed child a chance to be listened to one-to-one before any conflict arises.
- Explain boundaries clearly, with no more than three to five rules to give structure and security.
- Make sure that all helpers know fair and consistent consequences for breaking the rules. Consequences should not involve one-to-one attention as this may well be rewarding for a child and lead to more rule-breaking.
- Have your resources ready and have enough for all.
- Have some alternative activities ready in case what you planned is not engaging enough or at the right ability level.
- Set up the room so that each child has enough personal space.
- Be aware of your own level of self-control.
- Use words and body language that build empathy between you and the children.

Think about...
What rules and consequences do you currently use? Withdrawing privilege is a useful consequence; think about what privileges there are that you could withdraw.

Manage your own body language and words

Even if you are not feeling completely confident you can increase your appearance of calm confidence by unfolding your arms, opening your palms, relaxing your shoulders and your facial muscles and standing slightly sideways on. Breathe deeply and remind yourself that God thinks you are great.

Say 'thank you' rather than 'please', for example, 'Tim, I'd like you to come and sit with David, thank you'. This gives a feeling of expecting Tim to do this rather than 'please' which can sound like pleading. You might 'speak and spin', that is, make your request to Tim then turn away to other children. Again, this gives an air of confidence, and turning away means that Tim cannot see any hesitant body language on your part. If Tim does not sit down just repeat the same words, sometimes called the 'broken record' technique, but don't engage in debate about what you would like to happen.

Don't use 'why', it invites a 'because' response, which puts the child into defensive mode.

Try to avoid 'you' statements, they sound judgemental.

Three-part 'I' statements are a good way of putting your point of view without sounding blameful:

- 'I feel... (*upset*)
- when I... (*get interrupted*)
- because I... (*would like the group to hear the story about Jesus*).'

Think about...

If someone at home says, 'You never help with the washing up', how does that feel compared with, 'I would like it if I had some help to dry the glasses'?

In reality...

Susie had brought a packet of sweets and was throwing them one by one across the room. The leader looked across at her briefly, 'Susie, I wonder if you realised that I would like to finish the story first, then you might like to ask questions and you could reward the people who give the right answers'.

He turned facing slightly away from Susie and continued the story.

Susie started listening as she began to think of tricky questions to ask the other children. The group had a wonderful sweet-throwing time at the end of the session.

By pretending confidence and giving her some control over the activity, the leader improved their relationship. Now Susie will often approach him before the session to ask if she can 'do the questions' at the end.

Mood-matching

If empathy is present then two people will tend to copy body postures and voice intonations. Mood-matching is a method that uses this by copying the raised voice of the child who is agitated but uses positive language to gain a connection. 'I can see that you are upset. I want you to talk to me.'

This can also include matching body language, for example, marching around. Then the adult will gradually lower the tone and tempo and the child will 'come down' correspondingly.

Think about...

How annoying can it sometimes be if someone says 'calm down' in a controlled soothing voice when you are very wound up about something?

Reflective reframing

Reflective reframing aims to build in hope by suggesting that difficulties are temporary and solvable. For example, 'When you enjoy coming to church, what will be happening?' or 'When you are friends with Lucy, what will you do together?'

Think about...
What kinds of conflict have arisen, do or might arise in groups that you work with? What approaches from this chapter could you use to try and resolve the conflict? What is important about your own behaviour in conflict situations?

5 WORKING TOGETHER

If we want to see positive behaviour in our work with children and young people then we need to consider how we work with our team and the wider church. Often children's and youth work can feel a bit like the invisible man of the church – present but not always so that people are aware of it and what it is doing. But whether we feel it or not 1 Corinthians 12:27 states: 'Together you are the body of Christ. Each one of you is part of his body.'

Who's in the team?

It could be your team are the people who run the Sunday group when you aren't there, a group who run a club with you each week or the wider leadership of the church. So how can you work together better as a team and help each other out?

Who's the boss?

Every team needs a leader. This doesn't mean that they lead every activity, but just that they have overall authority. Having a leader can mean that there is clear communication to all involved. It can also mean that there is someone around with whom the buck ultimately stops. The leader needs to be someone who the children or young people know and respect. They need to know that the leader genuinely cares for them and wants the best for them. However, the leader also needs to be someone who can enforce any rules you have when it is necessary. Having an overall leader should take some pressure off the rest of the team members in terms of ultimate responsibility for working with difficult behaviour.

I'll watch your back…

It's pretty true to say that we all have our own areas of weakness and 'buttons' that can be pressed. What might really wind up one member of our team may not have any impact on another. This is where we need to support each other in our gifts and weaknesses. It could be that a young person's behaviour is really getting to you. Despite all your best efforts, you can feel yourself getting stressed.

Rather than trying to carry on like some kind of valiant hero, now is the time to get someone else to step in and deal with the situation. This doesn't mean that you have failed. If anything it shows that you have the strength to ask for help before you lose your cool. One way to support each other is to ask others to step in and take over when necessary. This should be agreed in advance amongst your team – that where one is struggling they can ask someone else to step in. It could almost be like a Christian tag team!

Wider support

Just as we need to be united in our support of others working with children or young people, so we too need to be working in alignment with the wider church that we are a part of.

We were all created to work together as part of Christ's body. Sadly, in some churches, the children's and youth work can operate almost as a separate unit from the rest of the church. This can be because the work that takes place is often out of sight of the wider church. Of course, this kind of situation couldn't be further from what God wants for us or for his church. The work with children and young people needs to be closely interwoven with the life of the church. Ideally, your church leadership should be aware of and in support of your rules, rewards and consequences.

Imagine the scene, you are running a midweek club and a child's behaviour becomes so bad that you have to ask them to have a few weeks off from the club. The child's father is incensed and comes down to the church building to 'have it out' with the church leader. The church leader knows nothing about your rules and assures the parent that 'it was probably just some kind of misunderstanding' and says the child can attend as normal. Inadvertently, the church leader has undermined the leader's authority. The team could be left with low morale and a gap between the leadership and church may begin to emerge. Equally, the team haven't informed the church leader of their rules or that a potentially difficult situation with the child's father may arise. The church leader has also been left in a vulnerable situation.

So, regular meetings with the church leadership are a must. This can be time to talk things through, pray together, talk about the future and coordinate things together.

Boundaries and consistency

Most people like boundaries and consistency. There can be nothing
worse than being told one minute to do one thing and the next being
told something else. Have you ever had the experience of getting lost,
asking for directions and someone telling you that one way is definitely
the right way? You get so far and then forget the second half of
directions so you ask someone else. However, the next person you ask
says you have come completely the wrong way and you should be
heading in the opposite direction. As someone who gets lost quite a
lot, I find myself getting more and more confused and more and more
wound up.

Imagine if you were someone attending the group you are involved
in. Different leaders have different boundaries on what is OK and not
OK behaviour. One week you arrive and you are expected to behave

In reality...

A church youth club ran each week in the local community. The group had a
set of rules and consequences that all who attended were aware of. One night
one of the young people broke one of the rules and the youth leader involved
followed the agreed consequence for that rule – they were told to leave the
premises. Not long after the youth leader saw the young person back in the
club – another leader had let them back in, saying that, 'It didn't really matter.'
The leader who had originally dealt with the situation felt undermined and the
relationship between the two leaders broke down. Over the following months
behaviour in the group went downhill as the young people realised that the
youth leaders could be played off against each other.

one way. Another week you are expected to behave in another. How would you feel? Would the shifting boundaries make you more or less likely to behave disruptively? Would you be able to play one leader off against another?

People (adults included) like consistency. They like to know where they stand and what is expected of them. So any rules or boundaries that you set up need to be the same week in week out – regardless of who is in charge that week. Of course, different people lead in different ways, but the rules or the foundations always need to stay the same. So, too, do the consequences of breaking (and keeping) the rules. By doing things this way the whole group becomes more stable. Everyone knows where they stand and you're more likely to have a positive time together.

So how do we set up rules, consequences and rewards?

Making the rules

If we want any rules to be kept then the first thing we need to think about is who is going to decide them. The more people that attend your activity and are involved in agreeing the rules, rewards and consequences, the more chance you will have of people keeping to what you have agreed.

Before involving the children or young people, you should first meet with any other adults involved and decide on the fundamental rules. This is to make sure that the essential points are covered when you meet together with your group. This time is also the chance to think of some possible rewards and consequences. These

> **Think about...**
> What sort of rules do you think are the absolute 'must haves' in a club or activity?

shouldn't be set in stone (otherwise there would be no point in consulting the children or young people) but will give you some ideas to start from if necessary. The emphasis should also be more on rewards than consequences.

Your next step to setting up rules is to meet with the children or young people. First you need to decide on the rules, next the rewards and finally consequences. The exercise shouldn't be too long but it should allow time for people to have their say. One way to do this is to split your group into smaller groups and then feed back the main ideas to the wider group. So each group may have five minutes to think about, 'What rules do we need in place to make this group the best it can be?' Try to make every idea positive. For example, rather than saying, 'Don't hurt anyone', make this into a positive statement, such as, 'Keep ourselves and others safe'. If they haven't already been covered, make sure that the ideas you have discussed as a team are fed in.

The final step is to hone down the ideas to just a few. Avoid a long list! If you have a list of twenty rules, people will probably not keep to them as it can all feel a bit overwhelming (and hard to remember!).

Think about...
Can you summarise your group rules in a list of five?

In reality...

A children's club was trying to put together a rewards system. The children immediately began to suggest ideas such as, 'If we are good for a week we all go to Disneyland.' After a fair amount of discussion, the leaders managed to negotiate the children down from Disneyland to a trip for everyone to a big theme park. However, to get the trip, they had to get stars for positive behaviour over a term and reach a combined target for the whole group. A grid was devised by the children whereby smaller rewards for good behaviour could be achieved along the way. They worked together and eagerly checked where they were on the chart each week. After a term, the children managed to achieve their trip to the theme park.

Repeat this process for rewards and consequences. When everything is done, either write the rules, rewards and consequences up and make sure they are displayed every week or, better still, get the children and or young people to do this. By involving them in as much as possible, these things become much less about you as a team imposing things on them as them belonging to the group themselves.

When we disagree

Most people have been in a situation where they see someone being dealt with in a harsher way than they think is necessary. Maybe you have seen an interaction and thought, 'I wouldn't have handled it that way.' If you have an agreed set of rules and consequences then the chances of there being a major disagreement are reduced greatly. Everyone should be dealt with in an equal way and in a way that has been agreed as fair.

However, if there are instances where there are disagreements amongst the team, it's essential that these are not brought up in front of the children or young people. Doing so allows the group to see division amongst the team (not a good role model) and increases the chances of one leader being played off against another. Any disagreements should be dealt with in private and after the event where possible.

When someone needs to be contacted
Perhaps the ultimate 'consequence' of not keeping to the rules may be that a child's parent or carer is contacted about their behaviour. This really is something that should be a last resort (decide together as a team what behaviours a parent or carer should be informed about). However, if things really are at the stage where someone else needs to be informed, it's important that this contact is made by the main leader of the group. The church leader should also be informed.

If the child or young person is a church member, then a quiet word after a church service should suffice. If possible this should be done

with the child or young person present (if they want to be). This way, they are not shut out of things and will have a chance to say what they think.

Think about...

What kinds of words might bring about a more positive reaction if you were speaking to a parent or carer about their child? What kinds of words might bring about a more negative reaction?

This sort of contact may be more difficult if the child or young person is not a part of the church. As before, the church leader should be informed. If you have a good relationship with the parent or carer, then the same approach should be taken as before. If not, then ring the parent or carer and discuss the issues with them over the phone – or offer to meet if the parent or carer would prefer. Most parents or carers are hugely embarrassed to hear their child has been in trouble and this may well come out as a defensive response. Try to not react to this. Stand your ground and acknowledge that it is a difficult situation for everyone. Emphasise how much you want the child or young person to do well and how difficult it was for you to come to this decision. Always explain very

Think about...

If we know we can only run a children's or youth club for the next six months, should we still do it? Is 'something better than nothing?' What sorts of things do you need to think about when considering this?

clearly *why* you have had to speak to them, and go through the specific things that have happened.

In for the long haul

As we have said earlier in this book, everything we do needs to be encased in God's love for those we work with. Rules and rewards are useless if they aren't motivated by God's love for a person. A fantastic way to communicate God's love is to continue to show that a child is valued no matter what they do. It means that we have a long-term commitment to the work we are involved in and the children, young people and team we meet there.

6 ADDITIONAL NEEDS

Sometimes leaders and helpers are concerned when they talk about children with special or additional needs, wondering about how they are going to connect with them. (Note: 'Additional needs' is increasingly used in schools and churches rather than 'special needs'.) But we all have needs and interesting quirks – it might be better to talk about 'us and us' rather than 'them and us'. For example, how many of us react badly to unforeseen change? Who among us gets bored easily and likes to change activity, doodles or fiddles with their pens? From God's perspective, don't we all have learning difficulties?

Many of the strategies suggested for working with children on the autistic spectrum will be effective for others who find change difficult. Similarly, ways of supporting children with ADHD (Attention Deficit Hyperactivity Disorder) can be helpful for the child (or adult) who finds it hard to sit still.

Terms used can change, but for the purpose of this book **learning disability** is defined as a difficulty in academic understanding. The term **learning difficulty** refers to an impairment of brain function resulting in one of the 58 (currently identified) conditions starting dys... (such as dyslexia and dyspraxia), or ADHD and other associated conditions. A child with a learning difficulty is often very bright, and the frustrations of the difficulty or difference may lead to challenging behaviours.

Learning disabilities

The most common additional need that you will encounter is learning disability. There are about 346,000 children with a learning disability in the UK (2005, Cabinet Office). Of those children, Down syndrome is the most likely form of disability; around 1 in every 800 live births is a child with this condition.

Down syndrome

Children with Down syndrome have a learning disability that may range from mild to severe. Be aware that ability can be very different on different days. Get ready with pictures, colouring and alternative activities if the child is not able to read or write. The children often have a degree of hearing impairment that also fluctuates on different days, so get eye contact before talking by using the child's name or touching briefly on the arm.

Many children will imitate other children's behaviour and enjoy sign language and imitating actions. Learn some sign language; check out the resources at the end of the book to discover how (page 79). Children with Down syndrome often tire easily as they do not always sleep effectively. They can forget instructions almost instantly and have a short concentration span. This can lead to emotional volatility. Give only one instruction at a time using short sentences. Have a place or a beanbag for the child to go and rest for a while.

If the child's speech is unclear, give them plenty of time to respond. Listen carefully and you will gradually understand more approximate words.

Give short, positive encouragements of the behaviour that is wanted in a calm voice; for example, 'Stuart, hands down please', rather than, 'Don't do that! Stop pinching Sophie!'

In reality…

Mitch always burst into the room at the start of a session with a big thumbs-up sign and ran over to his favourite helper to give her a cuddle. The helper started by accepting the cuddle and saying, 'Thank you, Mitch. 1, 2, 3… and away.' At this point she moved him gently but firmly away from her. She then asked for a 'high five', before giving him a picture timetable so that he knew what would be happening during the session. After a few sessions 'high fives' became the accepted greeting for not only Mitch but the entire group. The other children's willingness to learn some sign language boosted Mitch's confidence and lessened his need to run off crying or to demand physical contact.

Most children with Down syndrome enjoy tactile activities and can be caring and enjoy helping others. Sometimes this leads to more physical contact than is usual. Rather than pushing the child away in a flurry of anxiety about your church's child protection policy, it might be better to accept the child trying to cuddle you or climb onto your lap for a very short while so that the child does not feel rejected.

A child that has Down syndrome may also have other needs. Resistance to change may not just be about feeling tired, it may also be a reflection of being somewhere on the autistic spectrum or not being used to clear boundaries. Look at the chart in Part Three of this book. Pray and consider different strategies based on your knowledge of and relationship with each child.

Learning difficulties

Dyslexia

Think about...
Each child you work alongside is unique.
Difficulties do not usually come in neat
packages.

Many people who work with
those with dyslexia or Specific
Learning Difficulty (SpLD) use the
term 'learning difference'. Children will experience difficulty
with their short-term memories, they may forget what you have just
said, especially if you have given more than one instruction at a time.
They will have problems putting things in order: sounds, letters, words
and sentences. Some children feel that print looks 'wobbly', letters
seem to move around and they have difficulty reading words on a
page. Information may be processed more slowly, and organising what
equipment is needed for a particular activity may be difficult.

Such children are often very creative and have an ability to look at
things from different perspectives. Richard Branson and Albert Einstein
are among a whole host of exceptional people with this learning
difference.

However, research shows that many children with dyslexia suffer low
self-esteem and a lack of
confidence. Any church

Think about...
'In the beginning was the Word,
and the Word was not a book.'
How could you change activities
so that a child who struggles to
read will still take part
effectively?

session that relies heavily upon reading and writing may seem like a threat, and 'fight or flight' behaviours could emerge.

In church we are often much focused on books. Are there children in your church who 'forget' their Bibles, 'just have to pop to the loo' or rip up a worksheet saying 'this is boring' so they don't have to read anything?

Head off potential problems by making printed material as clear as possible. Keep font size to 12 or above, don't type in capital letters and use fonts without 'curly' bits such as Tahoma or Comic Sans. Use one and a half line spacing and put a small chunk of text and an illustration on each page.

Try other methods of learning. There is a whole series of Scripture Union books on multi-sensory ways of connecting with God (see Resources on page 79).

Low self-esteem and confidence are not fixed; we can experience the joy of seeing transformation as, with God's help, we find ways of enabling children to see their worth.

ADHD

More boys than girls are diagnosed with Attention Deficit Hyperactivity Disorder (ADHD). Around 70 per cent of those diagnosed are hyperactive and the other 30 per cent, who are mostly very easily distracted, are described as having Attention Deficit Disorder (ADD).

Children with these conditions have three areas of behavioural difficulty: impulsivity, inattention and hyperactivity.

In reality...

Thomas seems unable to stay in one place for any length of time or relate to other children without overreacting. He was running around at the back of a meeting, dashing out of one door and reappearing from another. His smaller brother took one of his shoes and also ran off.

Thomas started to cry loudly. The steward at the back of the meeting went to Thomas who, interestingly, agreed to pray with him. God intervened and Thomas began to calm down. He was then given the job of 'bouncer' at one of the doors. He carried out this role beautifully with a wide-legged, albeit only one-shoed, arms-crossed stance. His brother returned the other shoe as he realised the wind-up was not working, and Thomas continued to revel in having a special job.

Impulsivity

Being around someone with impulsivity can be unsettling. An idea that comes into the person's head is not processed but acted upon instantly. Peter the disciple seems to have been quite an impulsive man, for example: getting out of the boat to walk on water (Matthew 14:29); making impulsive suggestions at the transformation of Jesus (Matthew 17:4). Maybe he would have been given a label of ADHD today! Yet, in the end, Jesus gave him a key role in building the church (Matthew 16:18).

Strategies for supporting those who struggle with impulsiveness include:

Think about...

Which of the children you are alongside are over-impulsive? Which tend to blurt out answers and interrupt, and often have difficulty taking turns?

- Have clear, simple rules and expectations, for example: 'Jack, listen first, think of your answer and then put up your hand.'
- Don't try to correct all interruptions, decide to ignore minor inappropriate behaviour and be ready to praise when the child manages some self-control.
- Praise, also, when you see the child practising good social behaviour, such as letting another child have first go at an activity.
- Keep reassuring and encouraging each child.
- Focus on the child's talents.
- Avoid triggering 'fight or flight' behaviour by being aware of your use of language. Use 'I' statements rather than 'you' statements, for example: 'I would like you to sit down' rather than, 'You must... '.

Inattention

Children that have difficulty staying attentive may not seem to be listening when you speak to them. They may often have forgotten or lost items and can be very distracted by what is else is happening in the room.

Strategies for supporting those who struggle with inattention:

- Get eye contact before talking by using the child's name and then a short pause before giving an instruction, 'Lucy... Lucy, I would like you to come and sit near the others.'
- Give lots of regular praise while the child is doing the activity: 'Thank you, Lucy, you are sitting beautifully.' (Sometimes a small smile or 'thumbs up' between yourself and

the child achieves this without distracting other children and prompting a feeling that one child is getting more attention.)

- Encourage the child to sit by you and not too close to other children.
- Give the child something different to do if a reading or writing task provokes avoidance behaviour. 'Lucy, I have some picture cards of the story in this folder if you choose to sort them instead of doing the worksheet.'
- Encourage the child to have a checklist for what needs to be remembered.
- Keep your activities short.
- Give the child one instruction only at a time and use as few words as possible. It could be helpful for the child to repeat the instruction out loud. 'Lucy, can you repeat what I would like you to do, please?'

Hyperactivity

Children that are hyperactive will often fidget and run around when you would like them to remain seated. They may climb over furniture, talk all the time and find it hard to play quietly.

Strategies for supporting those who struggle with hyperactivity:

- Use activities that involve movement. Let the child be the one who writes on the flipchart.
- Have short breaks between activities.
- Give the child a 'concentrator'. This could be a purpose-made one from a company like Tangle Creations, or else it could be a stress ball, coloured paperclip or lump of playdough.

In reality…

David burst into the room and started 'investigating' the other children's property, clothing and hair. Each negative response from another child sent him off around the room again at full speed, his anxiety levels rising as his feelings of rejection increased.

The problem was solved by the leader setting up a concentration bag – a drawstring bag filled with interesting fiddly items. All the bag's contents were robust and quiet when played with. David learned to come first to the leader and spend time looking through the bag. He then chose one item that he kept with him until the end of the session. After a few weeks he always chose the same item, a battered plastic action man whose arms and legs could be constantly moved without disrupting the group.

Autistic spectrum disorders

The specific cause of ASD, Autism Spectrum Disorders, is unknown. Disability in the development of the brain affects a child's ability to communicate, understand language, play and interact with others. Autism becomes apparent before the age of three and affects more boys than girls.

Children with ASD vary a lot in ability and personality. They might also have severe learning difficulties or be bright and able.

Children with autism can prefer to be alone and tend to move away from other children and adults. They will be resistant to changes of activity or the layout of a room. Children with ASD may be hypersensitive to bright lights or loud noises. They may be undersensitive to pain or danger, for example holding hands under a tap with very hot water and suffering a scald because pain was not felt. You may also witness extreme tantrums when anxiety levels are raised

In reality...

Esme is unable to hold a conversation face to face. Her particular focus is hand-drying machines and a timed reward of going to the cloakroom to use a hand dryer will prompt positive behaviour. She also has a wonderful ability to pick out Christian songs by ear and play them on the piano in perfect tune. She repeats some of the words as she sits in her world connecting with God who loves her and can communicate in ways that we do not yet understand. It is a privilege to look beyond the unusual and sometimes difficult behaviours to see God building connections and using Esme to point those around her towards the kingdom.

too high. Most of these children have a particular focus of interest, such as lorries, and some will have amazing talent in a specific area, such as music or numbers.

Similar disorders

You may also meet children with diagnosis for:

Rett syndrome, which mostly affects girls and becomes more apparent with age.

Asperger syndrome, which describes children who have characteristics of autism and are academically able.

Childhood Disintegrative Disorder, which refers to children whose development appears normal for the first few years, but then falls back with the loss of speech and other skills until the characteristics of autism become clearly seen.

PDD-NOS, Pervasive Developmental Disorder – Not Otherwise Specified which is used to identify children who have some of the characteristics of disorders on the autistic spectrum but who do not fall into any of the existing specific cetegories of autism.

Strategies for supporting those on the autistic spectrum
- Get eye contact, if possible, before talking by using the child's name. Children may not give eye contact at all but may look at and respond to pictures, text, symbols, objects or puppets.
- Use signing, facial expression, gesture, text, pictures and objects to support communication, as a child may not be able to take in information by listening to spoken words.
- A child may be able to respond by writing, drawing, pointing to a picture or symbol, but not respond verbally.
- Use picture, word or symbol schedules to help the child understand and predict the sequence of activities.
- Give clear notice of change of activity. You might use ten fingers held up and count down, or a timer may be helpful.
- Give extra time for warning of changes from routine activities. You might say, 'In five minutes… ' then, 'In one minute… ', before the ten-finger countdown.
- Give opportunity for moving around and physical activity.
- A stress ball or 'fiddle' object may meet the need for activity so that the child may be able to access a story at the same time.
- Use a child's enthusiastic interest as a learning opportunity or as a reward for a task completed.
- Avoid triggering 'fight or flight' behaviour by being aware of sensory overload – noises,

lights, touch will seem far more loud, bright or unpleasant to the child than to you.

- Be aware of your use of language. Use 'I' statements rather than 'you' statements. For example, 'I would like you to sit down' rather than, 'You must... '.
- Some children may not have the concept of 'I' and 'you' and will need the sentence structure that very young children use, for example, 'Jack can have a drink now' rather than, 'You... '.
- Give only one instruction at a time using short sentences and visual prompts – signing, words, pictures as well as your voice.
- Be alert to a possible lack of awareness of danger – for example, hot radiators or roads.
- Provide structure and clear guidelines regarding your expectations for appropriate and inappropriate behaviour.
- Find opportunities to praise good behaviour, and ignore inappropriate behaviour if possible as giving attention to it may serve to reinforce it.
- Try not to intervene physically if sensory stimulation behaviour occurs. Some children may rock on their chairs or put their hands inside their trousers. Your touch may act as a threat. Try, 'Jack, hands on knees, thank you', or a traffic light 'red' picture.
- Have a calm place for the child to go that removes the threat of sensory overstimulation – some children like a fleece blanket to 'hide' under.
- A carpet square will sometimes encourage a child to sit in one place.
- A 'fiddle' box might be a reward or a timed chill-out activity.

- Give short positive encouragements of the behaviour that is wanted in a calm voice; for example, 'Stuart, hands down, thank you', rather than, 'Don't do that!' or 'Stop hitting'.
- Pray regularly for each child that you serve alongside.

There are very many other conditions that lead to behavioural challenges and this book cannot cover all of these.

There are also children who will benefit from some of the strategies suggested above even when they have no identified condition. Use the chart at the back of the book to identify possible ways of helping the child you work with to gain self-control and make good choices about behaviour.

Think about...
How could you use some of these strategies with the children or young people in your group?

In reality…

At each change of activity, Luke would scream loudly and put his hands over his ears. This happened both in church and in the children's groups. His mum began to think it was easier to stay at home than struggle to attend services. After a lot of discussion with Luke when he was away from church, he talked about it being 'too noisy' and that he was 'scared what is going to happen'.

Luke has been given ear defenders (big ones that sit around his neck for when he might need them) and a picture timetable with laminated pictures that he can alter around on a Velcro strip. The pictures include 'toilet' and 'drink' and 'beanbag' as well as 'Bible story', 'song' and other activities. Luke is able to feel in charge of what will happen by choosing the pictures and then removing them from the strip when he is forewarned that another activity will soon start. Both Luke and his mum are now happy to go to church and his behaviour at home can also be supported with other activity picture timetables.

PART THREE – PRACTICAL EXTRAS

3

My problem is...

My problem is...	Possible causes	Strategies
Angry outbursts	Feeling unloved Low self-esteem	Mood-matching (page 46) Partial agreement (pages 26 and 34) Anger diffusers (page 37)
Answering back Arguing	A perceived threat has triggered 'fight' behaviour	Manage your body language and choice of words (page 45) Active listening (pages 37 and 40)
Biting	Attention seeking Toothache	Behaviour plans (page 41)
Breaking things	Attention seeking Low self-esteem	Praise when OK (pages 21 and 64)
Can't concentrate Constant talking Does not seem to listen Fiddling with other children's stuff Fidgeting	Some form of hyperactive or attention deficit disorder	Look at strategies for ADHD and ADD (page 62)
Fighting with other children	A perceived threat has triggered 'fight' behaviour	Mediation (page 40) Reflective reframing (page 47) Circle of friends (page 42)

My problem is...	Possible causes	Strategies
Getting up and running around	Some form of hyperactive or attention deficit disorder	Look at strategies for ADHD and ADD (page 62)
General messing around Giggling inappropriately	Not engaged Fearful of being asked something difficult	Prepare alternative activities (pages 23, 44 and 65) Three-part 'I' statement (page 45)
Hitting out Ignoring spoken instructions	Some form of developmental disorder Lack of understanding	Strategies for autistic spectrum disorders (page 66) Total communication (page 68) Short sentences (page 59) Signing (page 59)
Inappropriate sexual behaviour	A distressed child Possible abuse	Record behaviour factually and talk with your church child protection officer; do not attempt to question the child yourself
Lying	Attention seeking Fear	Active ignoring (page 64) Three-part 'I' statements (page 45)
Physical contact	Often from children with Down syndrome	'1, 2, 3... and away' (page 60)

My problem is...	Possible causes	Strategies
Refusing to cooperate	A perceived threat has triggered 'fight' behaviour	Manage your body and language (page 45) Speak and spin (page 45) Broken record (page 45) Time out (page 26)
Running away Screaming Tantrums	Some form of developmental disorder	Strategies for autistic spectrum disorders (page 66)
Taunting other children	Inappropriately trying to make friends	Three-part 'I' statements (page 45) Reflective reframing (page 47)
Tearing up worksheets	Attention seeking Fearful of being asked something difficult	Look at strategies for dyslexia (page 61)
Uncooperative	A perceived threat has triggered 'fight' behaviour	Manage your body and language (page 45) Speak and spin (page 45) Broken record (page 45) Time out (page 26)
Unwilling to join in activity	A perceived threat has triggered 'flight' behaviour	Reflective reframing (page 47)

My problem is...	Possible causes	Strategies
Using swear words	Attention seeking habit Feeling threatened	Active ignoring (page 64) Self-calming (page 37)
Vandalism	Attention seeking Low self-esteem	Behaviour plans (page 41)
Whispering inappropriately	Inappropriately trying to make friends	Three-part 'I' statements (page 45)
Whingeing	Not engaged Fearful of being asked something difficult	Prepare alternative activities (pages 23, 44 and 65)
Something else?	See the behaviour as an unconscious cry for help from the child	Behaviour plans (page 41)

CHURCH BEHAVIOUR POLICY

An example:

Here at *** church we value every single child, young person and adult. Through all our relationships and activities we want every person to be safe, cared for and to know God's love. This behaviour policy aims to provide a framework where we can do just that.

We ask all parents and carers to read and sign this policy, and hand it in to the appropriate group leader.

1   The leaders aim to keep everyone safe from any kind of harm.
2   Leaders and attendees will look after the equipment and rooms they use.
3   Everyone is expected to speak to each other with respect. If a leader asks someone to do something, they will be expected to do it.
4   If a parent or carer isn't happy with something to do with the group, they are encouraged to talk to a leader about it. If they're still not happy they can talk to the overall leader and, if need be, to the church leader.
5   If a leader thinks someone in the group may be in danger, they may contact someone about it.
6   If the overall leader is concerned about an attendee's behaviour, they may speak to the parent or carer about it.
7   Outside the times of the activities, attendees are the responsibility of the parent or carer.

Each group will put together their own set of rules, rewards and consequences. These will fit within the seven areas above.

TEN TOP TIPS

- It's all about relationships. Make them, try to keep them, restore them.

- Stay calm, separate the behaviour from the child. It's not personal against you.

- 'Not in front of the children' – if you need to redirect a child try to do it one-to-one. Use positive sentences to explain the behaviour you would like to see.

- Be careful not to make the situation worse. Use 'I' statements.

- Understand the difficulty by talking with the child and their parents or carers.

- Be prepared for your session. Show respect, give the children choices.

- Give attention to good behaviour. Praise, praise, praise.

- Be clear about boundaries, ensure consistency between leaders.

- Be flexible, use circle time or a back-up when your plan is not engaging the children.

- Pray for each child that you work alongside.

RESOURCES

Useful websites

www.deafchristian.org.uk – signs and other resources
www.easyenglish.info – easy to read Bible resources
www.incentiveplus.co.uk
www.prospects.org.uk – helping those with learning difficulties know God
www.schoolswork.co.uk – anger management, self-harming information
www.scriptureunion.org.uk/enable – additional needs information
www.scriptureunion.org.uk/Light/WebResourcesDownloads/TrainingReso
urces/theGRIDtraining/43732.id – active listening
www.tanglecreations.com
www.widgit.com – symbols for understanding

Scripture Union books

Denise Abrahall, *Top Tips on Welcoming special children*, SU, 2005

Multi-sensory series
Ian Birkinshaw, *Together*, SU, 2005
Ian Birkinshaw, *Parables*, SU, 2006
Craig Borlase, *World*, SU, 2008
Mike Law, *Prophets*, SU, 2007
Dave Maclure, *Message*, SU, 2008
Wendy Rayner and Annie Slade, *Seasons*, SU, 2005
Sue Wallace, *Church*, SU, 2005
Sue Wallace, *Scripture*, SU, 2005
Sue Wallace, *Prayer*, SU, 2007
Sue Wallace, *Worship*, SU, 2009

Pretty much everything you need to know about... series
Wigley, *Working with under 5s*, SU, 2005
Draper, Franklyn and O'Shea, *Working with 5–7s*, SU, 2007
Saunders and Porritt, *Working with 8–10s*, SU, 2004
Williams and Stephenson, *Working with 11–14s*, SU, 2004

Other publishers
Joni Eareckson Tada, *Special needs special ministry*,
Flagship Church Resources, 2003
Heather Geddes, *Attachment in the classroom*, Worth Publishing, 2005
Annette Hames and Monica McCaffrey, *Special brothers and sisters*,
Jessica Kingsley Publishers, 2005
Anna Richards, *ADHD: A challenging journey*, Sage Publications Ltd,
2003
Alan Thompson, *Easy way guide to signing*, Jak Books Ltd, 2003
Pip Wilson and Ian Long, *The big book of blob feelings*, Speechmark
Publishing Ltd, 2008